The S[...]

JOY

*to encourage
and inspire*

JEAN
WATSON

Illustrated by
Jane Hughes

A LION BOOK

INTRODUCTION

Troubles seemed to have been coming, in Shakespeare's words, 'not single spies but in battalions'. And my internal barometer was registering 'heavy and overcast' most of the time. Joy seemed to have disappeared from my life and I needed it — oh, how badly I needed it!

This book, in the form of reflections on joy, says something about where I found it or it found me, and is amplified by wise and enjoyable snippets from fiction and non-fiction relevant to the theme. For I have come to the conclusion that joy is legitimate even in this flawed world, and that it can play a vital part in the progress towards wholeness in attitude, relationship and lifestyle which life under the sun of God's grace is all about.

Of course, books are no substitute for personal support and care, and they can be positively unsuitable for someone torn by the raw anguish of the first stages of major trauma. But they can — and I hope this book will — contribute later on in the healing process. For while joy tends to elude those who specifically chase it, it does come, often unexpectedly, in response to other pursuits and conditions, and not least to the honest facing of and dealing with the darker side of reality in and around us.

This book has something to say about joys which arrive in this mysterious paradoxical way, as well as about the delights by which, even in this complex creation, we are all surrounded. And my hope is that — shadows and all — it will be to many a path towards genuine, state-of-the-universe joy.

Jean Watson

JOY AND INNER FREEDOM

I love the story of the small child in class who, after repeatedly being asked to sit rather than stand, finally complied while saying mutinously, 'I'm sitting down on the *outside* but on the *inside* I'm still standing up!'

This illustrates delightfully that outward conformity does not necessarily indicate inner compliance! Only when inner and outward freedom are going in the same direction can there be joy in the enterprise. And *any* direction will not do. For freedom to be genuine, it must be exercised appropriately and lovingly. This, I think, means being free to be who I truly am, both as a human being and my unique self, within the framework of God's love and wisdom – which tells me to love my neighbour as myself.

Some hardly enjoy their freedom at all: they're too busy shooting themselves in the foot by trying to flout the order within which it exists. Others may not realize the immense variation that is possible within – indeed *because of* – that order.

Nature practically shouts out the message that God is a lover of variety. Scientists tell us that diversity is a hallmark of life and that there may still be another 30 – 40 million species to be classified.

The God who created that sort of a world surely wants us to enjoy difference and variation, and to express our own distinctive version of humanness. In fact it is his love, accepting us warts and all, which sets us free to do just that.

Stone walls do not a prison make,
    Nor iron bars a cage;
Minds innocent and quiet take
    That for a hermitage.

If I have freedom in my love
    And in my soul am free
Angels alone, that soar above
    Enjoy such Liberty.

Richard Lovelace

Where the spirit of the Lord is present, there is freedom.

From 2 Corinthians 4

RICHES OF THE IMAGINATION

Although the imagination can be a huge source of joy, I can also identify with the person who said, 'I've had a lot of bad things in my life, most of which have never happened!'

A concrete example of this was inadvertently provided by our son. As a small boy, he was once playing with friends when a child on a tricycle pedalled past him. At once our son cradled his foot in his hands and proceeded to hop about giving little 'ooh-aah's of pain.

'Did the boy run over your foot?' I asked, rather surprised, because it hadn't looked as if he had.

'No, but he might've!' was the reply. Such is the power of imagination!

Fortunately, the imagination can also transform apparently negative feelings and experiences into positive ones, turning a routine procedure into a celebration, the humdrum into an adventure. It is playful, inventive and creative, asking 'Why not . . .?' and 'What if . . .?' It sees a boiling kettle and dreams up a steam engine. A garment blowing in the wind becomes a balloon; a spider's web, a suspension bridge.

Stories, ideas, nature, music, art, experience – all these can provide the necessary 'food' and 'space' for the imagination. And bringing a thriving imagination to bear on all areas of our lives is a delightful way of infusing our work, play and relationships with creativity and joy.

Be glad, earth and sky!...
Roar, sea, and every creature in you;
be glad, fields, and everything in you!
The trees and woods will shout for joy
when the Lord comes to rule the earth.

From 1 Chronicles 16

The Fir Tree stood very straight and majestical, with its
dark branches vibrant, as it looked at the wonders, and the
little Tomtit gazed entranced.

He saw the moon sail along the sky like a splendid ship
and on the deck there was a host of shining angels with
trumpets and horns, singing and playing the heavenly
music, cold and clear and far away.

From *The Tomtit and the Fir Tree*, Alison Uttley

JUST FOR THE FUN OF IT

We can all get rather heavy and intense sometimes, and I know that I very much need the checks and balances of play: doing things simply because they are fun and light-hearted. I'm not just talking about holidays and necessary breaks from routine, but about celebrations, treats, surprises: a film, a play, a concert; a time for silly games or home-grown entertainment; a spontaneous party or a special meal.

Many of us become rather hung-up about doing things for sheer enjoyment – perhaps because of growing up with the notion, picked up from goodness knows where, if it's *not* enjoyable, it's doing you good. (And presumably vice versa!) Others, conversely, seem to have fallen for the opposite extreme. *Everything* ought to be fun – if it isn't, forget it, and if it is, go for it, grab yourself a good time.

Somewhere in between comes the best kind of play, the kind which has a sort of innocence but is by no means just for children. Such play also reflects something of joy's true essence – its eternal quality, its very unnecessariness, and its carefree exuberance.

It is ironic that play and playfulness are often the first things to get squeezed out of life when we are under pressure, because never are they *more* needed than at such times. Play is significant and even keeps us sane, not just because it's part of our nature, but also because it gives us a glimpse of the joy and creativity of God himself.

Whoever does not welcome the kingdom of God like a little child will never enter it.

Jesus' words, from Mark 10

Do something unusual. Be an experimenter . . . Let people think you're a loony. Wear a funny hat or put your shirt on backwards for a day . . . Hug a tree, fly a kite, wear a button, jog in triangles. Go for a long walk in your bare feet. Poke some holes in your rigidity.

From *When I Relax I Feel Guilty*, Tim Hansel

HEALING LAUGHTER

While there was nothing funny about my mother being very ill in hospital once, she inadvertently had her little corner of the ward falling about one day.

What happened was this. My mother, a missionary and vicar's wife, had for days been lying mute and withdrawn, with her eyes shut. A nurse's aide had come in and begun tidying the beds: a cheerful woman who chatted as she worked, dropping the odd casual 'bloody' here and there.

Suddenly a voice cut firmly across her monologue: 'Not so much of the "b"'s, thank you!' This was greeted, after a few seconds of stunned silence, by considerable mirth. The speaker, incredibly, had been my mother.

It was hard to believe she had spoken; nothing seemed to have changed. But now everyone knew that inside the shell of silence and stillness her spirit was very much alive and kicking. And the laughter had expressed both surprise and joy at that fact.

While cynical, cruel, and malicious jokes are alien to joy, there are many kinds of humour that are happy, harmonious and healing. Best of all is the laughter of delighted surprise when something unexpected but wonderful happens; of irrepressible joy when things go gloriously right – as if to say, 'Of course! This is how it should be!'

Sarah said, 'God has brought me joy and laughter.
Everyone who hears about it will laugh with me.'
From Genesis 21

When print is made to lean over, it is called hysterics.
A nine-year-old child

God is dead,
Sartre.
Sartre is dead,
God.
(Graffiti)

THE PARADOX OF SUFFERING

At school I would resolutely clamp my mouth shut when the others sang these hymnlines: *I thank Thee, too, that all our joys are touched with pain, that shadows fall on brightest hours, that thorns remain.*

Because I wasn't thankful for any of those things. I feel very much the same today. But I have learnt that out of the experience of suffering can come good: growth in patience and endurance, understanding and empathy; and growth in our capacity to appreciate life's true riches – love, faithful friends, beauty, creativity and 'all good gifts around us'.

Sometimes, however, no such good or joy is evident. Suffering can seem utterly pointless, indiscriminate and haphazard. One person's selfless and loving life may end in dementia, robbed of all quality. A second person for no obvious reason seems to have an easy passage through life, while a third is so bombarded by circumstance that total despair would hardly be surprising.

It is love that can create a path through even acute suffering, and make the mystery of suffering tolerable. It does so not by providing explanations, but by healing wounds and giving us reason and courage not just to survive but to take the risk of living fully again.

This transforming power applies both to human love and, even more, to God's love. He suffers with us and comforts us. And this subtle joy holds hands with hope. For God not only offers real consolation in the present, but also the assurance that one day, right and justice will prevail, and evil and suffering will be swallowed up in unshadowed joy.

The other gods were strong, but thou wast weak;
They rode, but thou didst stumble to a throne;
But to our wounds only God's wounds can speak,
And not a god has wounds but thou alone.

'Jesus of the Scars', Edward Shillito

Tears may flow in the night, but joy comes in the morning.

From Psalm 30

The day must come when joy prevails and all the makers of
misery are no longer able to infect it.

The Great Divorce, **C.S. Lewis**

Deep Fulfilment

Popular goals today include fame, success, prestige, status, wealth and power. But few can be winners in these stakes, and those who are don't seem to be any happier than the rest of us.

Why? Partly, I think, because in the scramble for this kind of success, personal relationships tend to go by the board. And without loved ones to enjoy and share with us, our rewards quickly lose their lustre. More importantly, we were made for greater ends than these, and deep down our disillusionment with material gain tells us so, if only we will listen.

Often, it takes a crisis to open our eyes to the fact that *our* 'fulfilment' and 'rights' cannot be divorced from other people's – and hence from mutual care and responsibility. So we can only receive personal identity, success, freedom, possessions or power when others fulfil their responsibilities – in love, care, service – towards us. And, of course, vice versa.

If, as I believe, God made us, then nothing less than his ultimate purpose will bring us true fulfilment. Whether we work in a shop or dig up roads, nurse the sick or study metaphysics, our goals, rewards and ambitions will only bring us joy when they have the love of God and neighbour at their centre.

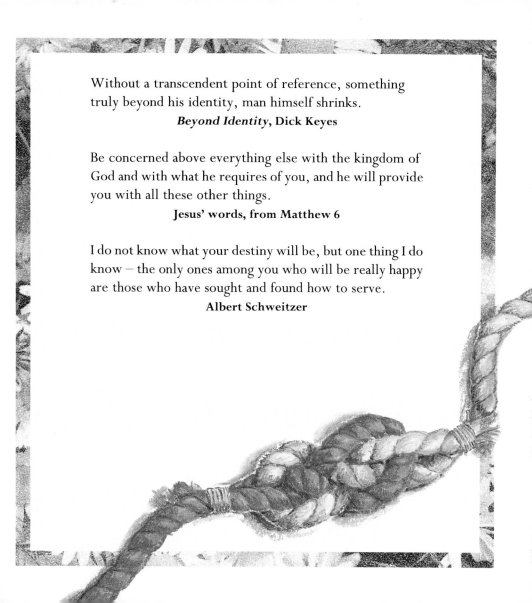

Without a transcendent point of reference, something truly beyond his identity, man himself shrinks.

Beyond Identity, Dick Keyes

Be concerned above everything else with the kingdom of God and with what he requires of you, and he will provide you with all these other things.

Jesus' words, from Matthew 6

I do not know what your destiny will be, but one thing I do know – the only ones among you who will be really happy are those who have sought and found how to serve.

Albert Schweitzer

EVERYDAY JOYS

Having someone from Africa staying in our home made me realize that one person's 'everyday' may be another's dream of bliss. Time and again he made us aware of how fortunate we are. Things which take us a few hours to sort out – tickets, banking and the like – would take him days of hanging around, not to mention the problem of bribery and corruption at all levels of officialdom. One day as we were unpacking our goods from the supermarket, our friend exclaimed without rancour, 'I envy you'. His eyes lit up at the very thought of being able to shop so companionably, conveniently and, from his point of view, so prodigally.

If we must make comparisons, it's only right to compare *downwards* as well as upwards, so as to 'get real' in our perspectives.

Trouble can be another more painful way of opening our eyes to everyday joys. For it is often when we feel weak and vulnerable, that the 'trivial round, the common task' provides the familiar, manageable framework and routines which steady and reassure us as we recover.

Once we start noticing them, simple joys seem to pop up all over the place: the aromas of hot bread, roasting meat, real coffee and fresh laundry; a clean and cosy room; colours of fabrics and flowers; spring sunshine after winter; a playful breeze.

These are gentle joys in their own right, but they also enhance more 'special' joys by providing contrast and balance – the latter being a key to unlocking many doors into enjoyment and wellbeing.

Look how the wild flowers grow: they do not work or make clothes for themselves. But not even King Solomon with all his wealth had clothes as beautiful as one of these.

Jesus' words, from Matthew 6

Sing hey! for the bath at close of day
   That washes the weary mud away!
A loon is he that will not sing:
   O! Water Hot is a noble thing!

The Fellowship of the Ring, **J.R.R. Tolkien**

NATURAL DELIGHTS

My study overlooks the back garden and as I write I can hear an outraged chirruping from a couple of highly indignant blackbirds. They believe they own the place and their space has been invaded by next door's elderly cat. If past experience is anything to go by, the intruder is about to be dive-bombed for his temerity.

On my desk lies a book about nature and, opening it, I am soon marvelling at the bio-luminescence of corals and the iridescence of the peacock's tail feathers.

In fact, the natural world is crammed with delights. The blaze of azaleas in full flower or the fragrance of jasmine and honeysuckle; the mischievous play of kittens or the rippling movements of squirrels along fences and up trees; the bloom on peaches, rose petals and children's cheeks, or the chuckle of a baby: it seems wasteful not to spend time enjoying any of these, and other soothing, stunning or stimulating joys.

Nature displays a staggering variety of structure and order, pattern and design. There is interaction, co-operation and hence community, as well as extraordinary differences in form, line, colour, sound, smell and function. There is growth and change – birth, development, death, new birth. Keeping a 'sense' diary is a way of heightening our joyful awareness of the sights, smells, sounds, textures and flavours around us.

Nothing in nature, of course, finally proves the existence of a creator. But it certainly doesn't disprove it either!

Ever since God created the world, his invisible qualities –
both his eternal power and his divine nature – have been
clearly seen; they are perceived in the things that God has
made.

From Romans 1

I taste a liquor never brewed.
From tankards scooped in pearl;
Not all the vats upon the Rhine
Yield such an alcohol!

Inebriate of air am I,
And debauchee of dew,
Reeling, through endless summer days,
From inns of molten blue.

'Inebriate', Emily Dickinson

CHECKING OUT ATTITUDES

Kill-joy attitudes

blinkered, closed

obsessively private, embarrassed

rigid, inflexible, invincibly right

hurried, thrown by delays

needing quick-fixes and neat
and tidy answers

self-obsessed

chronically self-pitying

hung up on rights and dues

categorizing 'them' and 'us',
exclusive

combative, threatened,
aggressive, spoiling for a fight

Joy-friendly attitudes

open, hospitable

welcoming, friendly

prepared to change, be wrong or
uncertain, ready to learn

able to wait and live with
unfinishedness

living with loose ends, partial
knowledge and mystery

aware of self (warts and all)

willing to risk a little objective
self-honesty

willing to be responsible

inclusive, welcoming others'
differences

at ease with oneself and others

Kill-joy attitudes	Joy-friendly attitudes
fanatical, dogmatic, opinionated	receptive, courteous, enthusiastic
bitterly resentful, remembering past offences	ready to forgive, and to forget
cynical, hard	trusting, vulnerable
hopeless and despairing, pessimistic, expecting the worst	realistically hopeful, positive, ready to look for a pin-prick of light
pressurized, driven, overwhelmed	standing back, playful, celebratory
nitpicking, demanding, discontented	affirming, tolerant, cheerful
grudging, possessive, mean	glad, generous, kindly, not counting the cost
traumatized, suffering loss	healed, aware of the love of others
afraid, unable to make decisions	confident, willing to act
self-hating, self-negating	self-understanding, self-accepting
no time, no room, no space	spontaneous, open to surprises, creative

THE JOYS OF FRIENDSHIP

More than anything else, friendship opens up the deepest joys: companionship; shared ideas and interests; being liked and wanted for ourselves; the freedom to share and communicate at many levels, to give and receive love, trust, affirmation, understanding, affection; the opportunities to play and work together.

In the closest partnership of all, that between a man and a woman, faithful love – though not in vogue these days – can produce those very special joys which shifting or impermanent liaisons can never generate: the fruits of long experience of and commitment to each other. The ones I value and wouldn't swap for any number of ecstatic moments are deep mutual knowledge of and access to each other; rock-solid trust and a sense of belonging; shared culture, memories, lore, humour; and rich levels and layers of human communication, exchange and interaction.

But there are many kinds of friendship: that of work colleagues, of siblings, of villagers having a good gossip, of team mates, of children at a playgroup. And in all these there is truth in the aphorism: if you want to have a friend, *be* one. Because the give and take between one person and another overlap so densely in friendship that, like the chicken and egg, it's hard to know – and doesn't really matter anyway – which came first.

Of course, nothing I do can win me friendship with God. But he offers it anyway, I believe – an altogether higher quality friendship, bringing correspondingly truer, deeper joys.

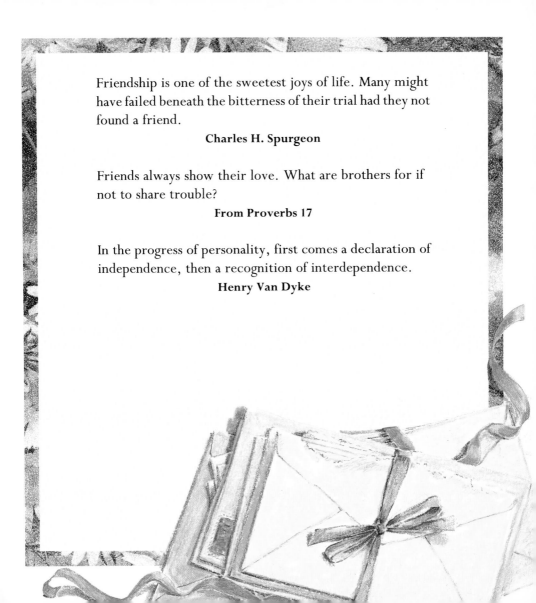

Friendship is one of the sweetest joys of life. Many might have failed beneath the bitterness of their trial had they not found a friend.

Charles H. Spurgeon

Friends always show their love. What are brothers for if not to share trouble?

From Proverbs 17

In the progress of personality, first comes a declaration of independence, then a recognition of interdependence.

Henry Van Dyke

COUNTING BLESSINGS

I know that the practice of counting blessings has gone out of fashion. But I've never set much store by fashion. And we may find it salutary, at times, to list on paper or in our minds the things we feel are against us beside what we've got going for us. I have often been touched and challenged when bereaved people have said to me things like, 'This is a terrible time, but friends have been wonderful,' or, 'At least I'm fortunate enough to have a home.'

A list of my pluses alongside the minuses nearly always prompts me to give myself a pep talk. When others attempt to buck me up in this way, they usually say the wrong things at the right time, or the right things at the wrong time – both of which are off-putting! But giving myself an objective talking to, when I'm good and ready, is another matter entirely.

This means telling myself how rich I am to have *any* let alone *many* of these: love, friendship, reasonable health, abilities, a home, access to nature, the chance to learn, develop, contribute, pursue interests, go on holiday, relax, have fun, travel. It also means facing the agonizing 'Why me? Why not them as well?' dilemma, so as to try to make the most of what I have, by enjoying it, managing it well, and sharing it freely.

Anything less than such appreciation and generosity would be churlish indeed. But, more importantly, joy returns in response to these attitudes. In particular, it grows as we develop a sense of gratitude towards all who enrich life, including, crucially, God – whose care and ordering of the world makes all such blessings possible.

I cried because I had no sandals
until I saw the man who had no feet.
Old Arab proverb

All shall be well, and all shall be well,
and all manner of things shall be well.
Julian of Norwich

WORKING IT OUT

Those who *have* work, never mind *enjoy* it, are very fortunate. But we do need to beware of workaholism – an addiction to which perfectionists and all artists are particularly vulnerable. There was a time in my life when the joy of writing and being paid for it went to my head. Then, one night, our son had a dream in which I was steadily typing while the house was in flames all around me. That was when I began to realize what I was doing.

The problem is that treating every interruption with happy acceptance, as an opportunity to be grasped, could make it difficult to work at all, let alone achieve excellence. On the other hand, a ruthless attitude brings a lack of balance and leaves no room for flexible, spontaneous responses of compassion or generosity.

As I was writing this, our neighbour rang in great excitement to discuss the ending of Shakespeare's *The Tempest*. He's over ninety, very lame and almost blind, but his enthusiasm for ideas is staggering. I would hate to miss interruptions like these.

In terms of a balanced, joyful lifestyle, work must never be at the expense of our all-important loving relationships. That apart, it can nevertheless channel our abilities into thinking big, taking affectionate care over detail, collaborating with others, learning new things, being stretched, getting a good result, and serving others. And in all these ways, joy can, and will, be found.

Nothing great was ever achieved without enthusiasm.
Ralph Waldo Emerson

Oh, you gotta get a glory in the work you do,
   A hallelujah chorus in the heart of you.
Paint or tell a story, sing or shovel coal,
   But you gotta get a glory or the job lacks soul.
Anon

God looked at everything he had made,
and he was very pleased.
From Genesis 1

NO STRINGS ATTACHED

Thanks to the popular image of a 'do-gooder', joy and 'doing good' almost sound mutually exclusive. But they needn't be. I don't know anyone who doesn't find some joy from being able to contribute to others, to share, lighten loads and relieve suffering. The benefits and joys received often seem out of all proportion to that which has been given.

At the very least, being able to serve someone else well makes humanity's sad music a little less unbearable. More importantly, learning to help one another is going to have to be the name of the game at every level – personal, local, international, global – if human beings are to survive, let alone thrive.

So why the bad publicity? I think it's because not all 'helping' does much, if any, real good! Mixed motives are something we all have to live with, but if the main ingredient is self-display ('Aren't I kind and good?') or self-interest ('You scratch my back, I'll scratch yours'), the effect can be crippling. Add to that an officious, patronizing or self-righteous manner, and you have the opposite of genuine, joy-spreading goodness.

When I feel I have nothing to offer, or so little that it seems negligible in the face of such vast need, I try to remind myself that improving things for even one person, without strings attached, has to be better than doing nothing for anyone; and that this way society changes – little by little, and person by person.

He who would do good, must do it in minute particulars.

William Blake

Do for others just what you would want them to do for you . . . Love your enemies and do good to them; lend and expect nothing back.

Jesus' words, from Luke 6

You must give your burden to someone else, and you must carry someone else's burden . . . I'm sure that this is a law of the universe, and not to give up your parcel is as much to rebel as not to carry another's. You'll find it quite easy if you let yourself do it.

***Descent into Hell*, Charles Williams**

THANKS FOR THE MEMORY

Remembering happy times, maybe with the help of photo albums and other mementos, can be a way into a more joyful frame of mind in the present.

I realize it doesn't always work this way. Some may feel worse rather than better, as they recall, accurately or nostalgically, a 'golden' past which seems to eclipse the present. Others may be confronted by unhappy memories – times they felt unlovable, afraid and helpless; when they were belittled, misunderstood, misjudged, mistreated.

But the answer isn't to block out the past. No-go areas in our memories probably indicate wounds that need attention and healing. And wise, trusted friends or counsellors can assist in both.

Within this therapeutic context, the self-discipline and pain of honest listening – to ourselves, to others and in particular to God – can lead to considerable relief and joy. As the past is laid to rest and all who caused its pain and problems are forgiven – including ourselves – we can approach the future with greater freedom and assurance.

One way of making the most of memories is to write them down as part of a personal joy list or scrapbook which we keep updating. In it we can record, for example, amusing or happy events, activities, or conversational snippets; the names of the people whose company we've enjoyed; and even the positive aspects of sad memories, such as the friends who stood by us and the points of learning and growth.

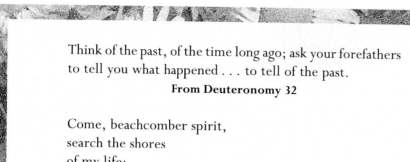

Think of the past, of the time long ago; ask your forefathers
to tell you what happened . . . to tell of the past.

From Deuteronomy 32

Come, beachcomber spirit,
search the shores
of my life;
bring to remembrance
love's presence.

Sister Gillian Mary

Humanity does not pass through phases as a train passes
through a station: being alive, it has the privilege of always
moving yet never leaving anything behind. Whatever we
have been, in some sort we are still.

C.S. Lewis

PRESENT JOYS

Many people find an increase in joy by learning to live a day at a time, giving themselves to the present moment and task. What prevents us from living like this? I think the main cause is anxiety, a mind-set of worry. And the antidotes? We find them in learning to trust – ourselves and above all God – and learning to deal with things and then leave them.

Trust and decisiveness in thought and action are not easy for those of us with a tendency to agonize! And in any case, a totally stress-free, worry-free existence is a pipe-dream. We are imperfect human beings living in an imperfect world where worrying things happen. Even so, people can and do find ways of making the most of each day, savouring its joys, facing its challenges, and taking to heart the 'sacrament of the present moment'.

Once, on a journal-writing course, a group of us looked back over our lives, identifying the plots, sub-plots and recurrent themes. Then, having discerned meaning and shape in our past, we were asked to identify where we were in the present by finishing these sentences: 'It is too late for . . .', 'It is too soon for . . .', 'It is just right for . . .'.

Reflecting on our present may make us face things that are far from joyful. Insights rarely come cheap, and meaning may need to be mined from the depths rather than gleaned from the surface. But making deep, lasting sense of our personal stories, which entails seeing them in relation to the Big Story, brings the kind of joy that makes life in the present worth living to the full.

Do not worry about tomorrow; it will have worries
enough of its own.

Jesus' words, from Matthew 6

Your attitude towards life in general is reflected in your
response to the dawn of a new day.

J.N. Gehman

JOYS TO COME

Often a way out of boredom and staleness is to start something new: take up a sport or other interest, join – or even start – a club or group, enrol on a course.

But it's important to distinguish between this kind of enlargement and escapism: a panic-stricken fleeing from one bolt-hole to another. Only by facing what needs to be dealt with at the right time – laying the past to rest and tying up loose ends – do new beginnings become genuinely possible, let alone potentially joyful.

The world of nature constantly points to the possibility of new beginnings and growth. Decaying matter – of the right sort and properly treated – plays a necessary part in the order of things. Perennials 'die' and bloom again. Spring follows winter. Life follows death.

I believe all this reflects something of God's nature. And it encourages me to keep trusting and co-operating with him as he continues his creative, regenerative work. Joy at its deepest is being part of what he is doing: bringing good out of evil; forgiving, revitalizing and energizing; and weaving the past into new beginnings and a positive future.

'Tomorrow the adventure begins anew,' Hodgkins continued. . .

'Not tomorrow, tonight!' shouted Moomintroll. And in the foggy dawn they all tumbled out in the garden. The eastern sky was a wonderful rose-petal pink, promising a fine, clear August day.

A new door to the Unbelievable, to the Possible, a new day that can always bring you anything if you have no objection to it.

The Exploits of Moominpappa, Tove Jansson

At any moment an unsatisfying life may become once more a grand adventure if we will surrender it to God.

The Adventure of Living, Paul Tournier

THE REAL THING

A group of students was gathered in our home, discussing their beliefs. One student was arguing that it didn't matter what you believed as long as you were sincere. Another stood up and addressed a question to the speaker. If he were to drink poison not knowing it was poison, would the poison kill him? The speaker did his best to brush this aside and resume his theme. But the questioner was not to be put off. He kept rising to his feet to reiterate with patient persistence, 'Excuse me, please, but will the poison kill you?'

In the end, the speaker admitted that yes, if he drank poison without realizing it, it would nevertheless kill him. And he and everyone else saw the point. Sincere belief is not all that matters. Reality can break in to reveal sincerely held beliefs as illusion.

For me, only joy that is reality-based is worthy of the name. It may feel euphoric to block out, or try to, what is evil and ugly and sad in ourselves and our world. But while choosing to live by the best and most enduring values, we must take account of both the pleasant and the unpleasant if we are to find true joy.

Over time, life's storms and winds blow away whatever is flawed or trivial. We need to redraw our maps of reality accordingly. This is not an easy or painless exercise, but there is joy in it. And every now and again, we sense our present reality being infused by ultimate truth, through God's extraordinary compassion, presence and activity.

Do not conform yourselves to the standards of this world,
but let God transform you inwardly by a complete change
of your mind. Then you will be able to know the will of
God – what is good and pleasing to him, and is perfect.

From Romans 12

. . . And please take care of yourself, God, because if
anything happens to you, we're done for.

A child's prayer

LIVING IN HOPE

One of the things I love about young children is their transparency, as shown in this letter written by a small boy to his aunt: *I am sorry I forgot your birthday. I have no excuse and it would serve me right if you forgot mine which is next Friday.*

As we grow older we become less transparent and also, perhaps, less hopeful. In fact, confronted by the crises, disasters and tragedies that make up much of the news, we could easily lose hope altogether. Of course, it's right that we should be aware of and responsive to the bad news. But we also need a balance, through focusing on and being encouraged by the good news as well.

After all, the world is full of amazing and felicitous 'coincidences' such as near-disasters 'miraculously' averted; and of mostly unsung heroes: people who behave selflessly or who reach rock-bottom but refuse to stay there, and who proceed to overcome the most appalling odds; who forgive others and rebuild shattered minds and bodies.

Being hopeful on that basis does lift our spirits, and there is no doubt about it: joy needs this kind of everyday hope. But perhaps we must go further. More solid and lasting joy needs more solid and lasting hope, something which will come only as we wrestle with eternal values. And as more profound hope begins to grow, so too does the potential for widespread positive change.

The bad news is: ours is an arduous, long and sometimes tedious journey through Cesspool Cosmos. And observe, it is a walk, not a sprint. The good news is: we are not alone on this demanding pilgrimage, which means that some folks we are travelling with make awfully good models to follow. So, follow them!

Laugh Again, Charles R. Swindoll

This hope does not disappoint us, for God has poured out his love into our hearts by means of the Holy Spirit, who is God's gift to us.

From Romans 5

Death is not the end . . . Death is only putting out the lamp at the rise of a new dawn.

Fear No Evil, David Watson

AT THE HEART OF IT ALL

Relationships are our greatest sources of both joy and pain, and either way, love is the key. It is the love in a relationship that creates joy; but when things go wrong, as they do, it is love that turns them round again.

Love is no quick or easy fix, however. When we fall out with someone, there is hurt and anger between us. We need time to handle these feelings and we need honest dialogue both with ourselves and with the other person. Love means admitting our part in the situation, and offering and receiving forgiveness. It also means being willing to risk friendship and openness again.

Restored harmony is a joy to experience, and in the process of attaining it, we are likely to grow considerably. We may develop greater self-control, or come to see our concerns more objectively. We may be able to put ourselves in the other person's shoes, and become a little more generous and humble. Of course, we all fall short. But if we recognize our inadequacy, we can then draw on God's perfect love and start to change our fraught lives, little by little, for the better.

If this applies at a personal level, it can also apply at the global one. Love breaks down social barriers, it links political prisoners, it builds bridges between different cultures and races, it chooses to care more deeply for our world. The love of God knows no bounds. We can therefore continue to grow in love – and our lives, relationships and activities can be increasingly characterized by wholeness and joy.

Love is patient and kind… is happy with the truth… Love never gives up; and its faith, hope and patience never fail.

1 Corinthians 13

We cannot avoid the love of God because it extends to each of us, his creatures. We can choose not to respond to it; in which case we can attempt love in our human fashion. Alternatively, we can respond to his love; and if we do, we can let him teach us more and more of what loving with the love of God means.

***Unafraid to Be*, Ruth Etchells**

The love for my own self is inseparably connected with the love for any other being.

Erich Fromm

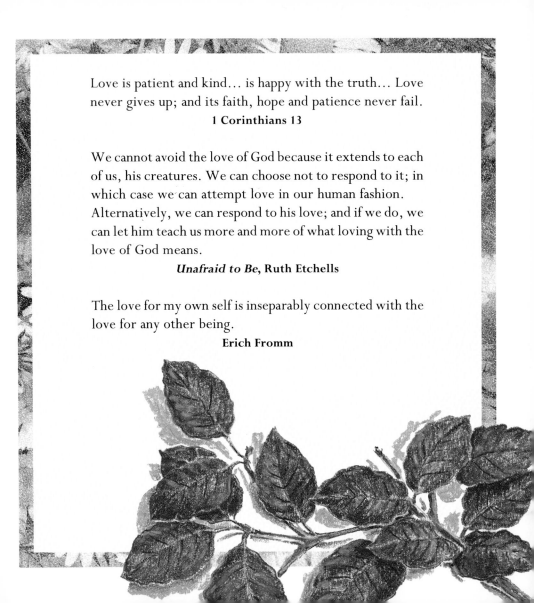

SECURITY

Understanding choice friendship

TRUST B·A·L·A·N·C·E LOVE warmth

Happiness Accord Blessing

TRANQUILLITY

Freedom JOY SURPRISE!

MATURITY harmony

Zest cheer

peace C·A·L·M Life Enthusiasm

HONOUR

BLISS Delight

comfort pleasure QUIET

FRESHNESS TENDERNESS

Laughter GROWTH fruition

HEALTH sunshine